Pacific Harbor Seal (*Phoca vitulina richardsi*) Monitoring at Point Reyes National Seashore and Golden Gate National Recreation Area

2011 Annual Report

Natural Resource Technical Report NPS/SFAN/NRTR—2012/611

Sarah Codde, David Press, Dale Roberts, and Sarah Allen

Harbor Seal Inventory & Monitoring Program
Point Reyes National Seashore
1 Bear Valley Road
Point Reyes Station, CA 94956

August 2012

U.S. Department of the Interior
National Park Service
Natural Resource Stewardship and Science
Fort Collins, Colorado

The National Park Service, Natural Resource Stewardship and Science office in Fort Collins, Colorado publishes a range of reports that address natural resource topics of interest and applicability to a broad audience in the National Park Service and others in natural resource management, including scientists, conservation and environmental constituencies, and the public.

The Natural Resource Technical Report Series is used to disseminate results of scientific studies in the physical, biological, and social sciences for both the advancement of science and the achievement of the National Park Service mission. The series provides contributors with a forum for displaying comprehensive data that are often deleted from journals because of page limitations.

All manuscripts in the series receive the appropriate level of peer review to ensure that the information is scientifically credible, technically accurate, appropriately written for the intended audience, and designed and published in a professional manner. This report received peer review by individuals who were not directly involved in the collection, analysis, or reporting of the data, and whose background and expertise put them on par technically and scientifically with the authors of the information. Data in this report were collected and analyzed using methods based on established, peer-reviewed protocols and were analyzed and interpreted within the guidelines of the protocols.

Views, statements, findings, conclusions, recommendations, and data in this report do not necessarily reflect views and policies of the National Park Service, U.S. Department of the Interior. Mention of trade names or commercial products does not constitute endorsement or recommendation for use by the U.S. Government.

This report is available from the San Francisco Area Network Inventory and Monitoring website (http://science.nature.nps.gov/im/units/sfan) and the Natural Resource Publications Management website (http://www.nature.nps.gov/publications/nrpm/).

Please cite this publication as:

NPS 641/116303, 612/116303, August 2012

Contents

Figures

Tables

Abstract

Pacific harbor seals (*Phoca vitulina richardsi*) are the most abundant and only year-round resident pinniped in the San Francisco Bay Area, California. Long-term monitoring studies have been conducted intermittently at the largest harbor seal colonies in Point Reyes National Seashore since the mid 1970s by various groups. The objectives of monitoring each site and the population as a whole are to i) detect changes in population size, ii) detect changes in reproductive success as indicated by pup production, and iii) identify anthropogenic or environmental factors that may affect the condition of the population (Adams et al. 2009).

Harbor seal surveys were conducted throughout the 2011 breeding and molting seasons (March-May and June-July, respectively) once to twice per week at the largest Point Reyes National Seashore and Golden Gate National Recreation Area harbor seal colonies, collectively referred to as Marin County locations. Members of the Harbor Seal Monitoring Volunteer Program helped to complete 224 surveys at eight Marin County locations, contributing an estimated 442 hours. During the breeding season, 2,676 adult and immature seals and 1,302 seal pups were counted at all Marin County monitoring locations. Drakes Estero had the most adult and immature seals (715), followed by Double Point (587). Drakes Estero and Double Point accounted for 59% (770) of pups at Marin haul-outs. During the molting season, 2,883 animals were counted at Marin County locations. The maximum pup count was above the mean count of the monitoring program's 12 year period; however, the molting season maximum count was one of the lowest recorded. During surveys, 94 disturbances to seals were recorded. The most frequent causes were humans on foot (29%), motorboats (21%), and unknown (20%). Twelve regional surveys were conducted throughout the breeding and molting seasons at locations in Sonoma, Marin, San Francisco, and San Mateo counties. Of these counties, Marin County locations accounted for 69% of breeding season adult and immature animals, 84% of pups, and 65% of seals during the molting season.

Acknowledgments

We thank all the volunteers who hiked many miles through fog, rain, and wind to survey harbor seals, including K. Aber, S. Andryk, K. Borden, D. Broderson, C. Campbell, K. Carolan, B. Carter, R. Catlin, L. Davidson, B. Felix, J. Ford, J. Forsell, A. Freeman, H. Grover, W. Holter, K. Irish, L. Johnson, J. Khudyakov, E. Kim, K. Kirk, T. Kirschner, J. Lamphier, E. Leite, D. Lingelser, D. Loeffler, B. Lutes, K. Mazzoni, D. McConnell, S. Pender, E. Podgurski, J. Sherman, S. Shpak, B. Siegel, E. Sojourner, J. Thompson, S. Van Der Wal, E. Vermeulen, S. Waber, A. Walker, K. Williams, and D. Winters. We are especially grateful to C. Campbell who not only conducted surveys but also assisted in training.

We also thank the regional group of volunteers associated with various collaborative groups, including N. Bell, S. Bush, M. Cooper, S. DeSilva, M. Engelbrecht, M. Follis, D. Greig, L. Kelsey, S. Lenz, K. Lindquist, S. Manugian, J. Mortenson, B. Plakos, B. Prochazka, J. Roletto, T. Seher, J. Sones, B. Wilson, L. Young and other agencies and organizations including the US Fish and Wildlife Service, Moss Landing Marine Laboratories, University of California at Davis, Farallones National Marine Sanctuary Association, Fitzgerald Marine Reserve, The Marine Mammal Center, and Stewards of the Coast and Redwoods Seal Watch program for contributing numbers to the region-wide surveys.

Finally, we are grateful for the generous contributions from the Point Reyes National Seashore Association, the David and Vicki Cox Family Foundation, and the San Francisco Bay Area Inventory and Monitoring Program.

All monitoring activities were conducted under the National Marine Fisheries Service Permit 373-1868-00.

The following peer reviewers greatly improved this document: Denise Greig and Marie Denn.

Introduction

The mission of the National Park Service is "to conserve the scenery and the natural and historic objects and the wild life therein and to provide for the enjoyment of the same in such manner and by such means as will leave them unimpaired for the enjoyment of future generations" (NPS 1916). To uphold this goal, the Director of the NPS approved the Natural Resource Challenge to encourage national parks to focus on the preservation of the nation's natural heritage through science, natural resource inventories, and expanded resource monitoring (NPS 1998). The NPS Inventory and Monitoring Program, initiated through the Challenge, is organized into 32 inventory and monitoring networks

The San Francisco Bay Area Network (SFAN) includes sites such as Golden Gate National Recreation Area, John Muir National Historic Site, Pinnacles National Monument, and Point Reyes National Seashore. The network has identified vital signs, indicators of ecosystem health, which represent a broad suite of ecological phenomena operating across multiple temporal and spatial scales. Our intent is to monitor a balanced and integrated set of vital signs that meets the needs of current park management, but will also be able to track unanticipated environmental conditions in the future. Pacific harbor seals represent a high priority vital sign for SFAN because they are ecologically significant, have protected status through the Marine Mammal Protection Act, and are of high interest to the public (Adams et al. 2006; Adams et al. 2009).

Harbor seals were also identified as a marine mammal species most likely to benefit from the establishment of marine protected areas (MPAs) in the north central California coast region under the Marine Life Protection Act (CDFG 2009). Five MPAs were selected within Point Reyes National Seashore along with three special closure areas where harbor seals may benefit. The MPAs were implemented in 2010 by the California Department of Fish and Game in cooperation with the National Park Service and monitoring data collected on harbor seals under this program may contribute to the assessment of the efficacy of the MPAs.

The information presented in this report is a summary of the harbor seal data collected at Point Reyes National Seashore and Golden Gate National Recreation Area during the 2011 breeding and molting seasons, March-July. Summary data collected as part of a region-wide survey effort, including adjacent areas (San Francisco Bay, San Mateo County, and Sonoma County) where NPS surveys were conducted in conjunction with other agencies and organizations for 2011, are also presented. This report is not intended to analyze long-term trends in the harbor seal data set, which are more appropriately investigated at five year intervals (e.g., Allen et al. 2004) or in scientific, peer-reviewed papers (Becker et al. 2011).

Background

Pacific harbor seals (*Phoca vitulina richardsi*) are the most numerous and only year-round resident pinniped in the San Francisco Bay Area, California. The population at Point Reyes National Seashore represents the largest concentration of harbor seals in the State of California, and accounts for approximately 20% of the mainland molting population (Lowry et al. 2005). Much of the Point Reyes coastal zone remains relatively undeveloped and provides good marine and terrestrial habitat for seals to rest, molt, feed, and breed where human encroachment is minimal (Figure 1). The inaccessibility of much of the area has historically afforded some protection from human disruption during the seals' terrestrial resting periods; however, some pinniped populations in California are still recovering from a long period of exploitation that did not end until the passage of the Marine Mammal Protection Act in 1972 (Sydeman and Allen 1999). National Park Service (NPS) is charged with managing and minimizing disturbance to pinniped habitat and activities from the more than 2 million annual visitors at Point Reyes and several million visitors at Golden Gate National Recreation Area (NPS 2010). The parks may implement visitor management actions to reduce disturbance to seals at colonies, if appropriate.

Objectives

Long-term monitoring studies of harbor seals have been conducted intermittently at the largest colonies in Point Reyes National Seashore since the 1970s (Chan 1979, Allen and Huber 1984; Allen et al. 1989; Sydeman and Allen 1999; Allen et al. 2004). The objectives of monitoring each site and the population as a whole are to i) detect changes in population size, ii) detect changes in reproductive success as indicated by pup production, and iii) identify anthropogenic or environmental factors that may affect the condition of the population. The monitoring objectives and protocol are described in detail in the San Francisco Bay Area Network Pinniped Monitoring Protocol (Adams et al. 2009).

Figure 1. The remote beach of the Double Point harbor seal colony at Point Reyes National Seashore. NPS Photo.

Methods

Study Area

The study area extends from Tomales Point to San Francisco Bay (Figure 2). The Point Reyes peninsula extends from the mouth of Tomales Bay (Lat. 38° 30'N) south to Bolinas Lagoon (Lat. 37° 30'N). Point Bonita is located in the Marin Headlands, at the mouth of San Francisco Bay in the Golden Gate National Recreation Area. For this paper, the Point Reyes sites and Point Bonita are collectively referred to as Marin County locations. Point Reyes National Seashore, Golden Gate National Recreation Area, Gulf of the Farallones National Marine Sanctuary, the California State Parks, and the county parks share jurisdiction over segments of this coastline, but overall, NPS lands account for most of the shoreline.

The topographic diversity of this coastal zone provides a broad range of substrates for harbor seals to come ashore. These include tidal mud flats, offshore and onshore rocky tidal ledges, and sandy beaches. A "haul-out site" is defined as a terrestrial location where seals aggregate for periods of rest, birthing, and nursing of young (Harvey 1987; Thompson 1987). Each colony site, or location, is comprised of several "subsites", or distinct areas of beach, rock outcrops, or sandbars where harbor seals haul out. Coastal embayment sites include Tomales Bay, Drakes Estero, and Bolinas Lagoon. Coastal sites surveyed include Tomales Point, Point Reyes Headlands, Duxbury Reef, Double Point, and Point Bonita (Figure 2).

Sampling Design

The current distribution of the harbor seal breeding population allows surveyors to monitor all breeding sites in Point Reyes National Seashore and the Golden Gate National Recreation Area. Thus, spatial stratification or other sampling techniques were not needed to decide which haul-outs to include for monitoring. Survey frequencies and timing capture the date of the first pup, the peak of the breeding and molting seasons, and have been shown to have sufficient ability to detect meaningful population changes over time. The main parameters monitored are reproductive success, population size, distribution, phenology, and disturbances (Adams et al. 2009).

The sampling design for this program enables the data to be integrated with other regional surveys, allowing for the results to be interpreted in a regional context. Annually, the National Park Service participates in regional harbor seal surveys during the breeding and molting seasons, with the Point Reyes National Seashore coordinating the central California coast surveys. Regional survey sites include colonies in Sonoma County (Sea Ranch, South Sonoma sites, Jenner, and Bodega Marine Reserve), San Francisco Bay (Castro Rocks, Alcatraz, Yerba Buena Island, Mowry Slough and Newark Slough), and San Mateo County (Fitzgerald Marine Reserve, Point San Pedro, Cowell Ranch Beach, Pescadero, Pebble Beach, and Bean Hollow) (Figure 2).

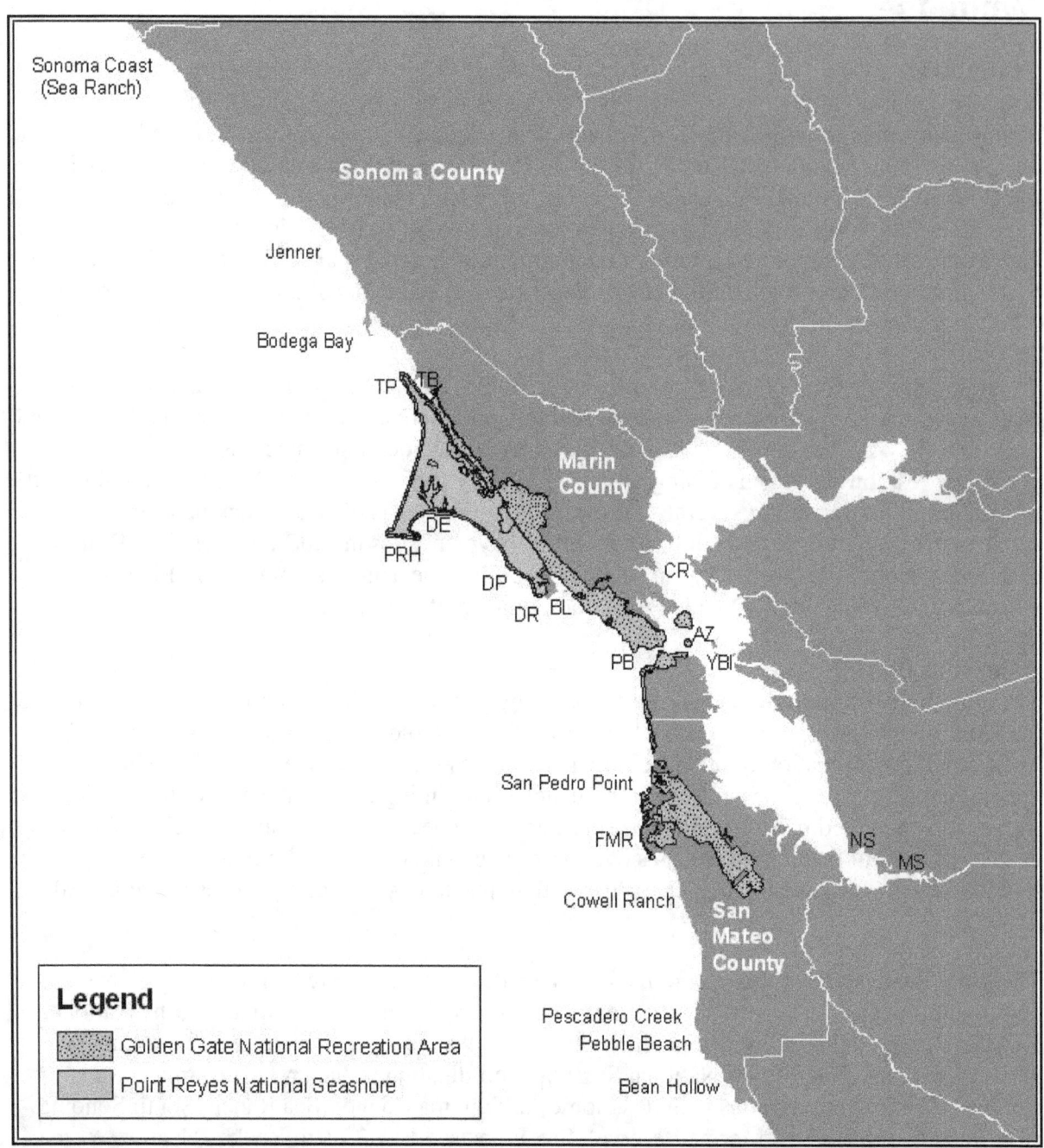

Figure 2. Regional survey sites in San Francisco Bay and Sonoma, Marin, and San Mateo counties, California. Map does not present all of the regional survey locations included in Sonoma and San Mateo counties. TB=Tomales Bay, TP=Tomales Point, DE=Drakes Estero, PRH=Point Reyes Headland, DP=Double Point, DR=Duxbury Reef, BL=Bolinas lagoon, PB=Point Bonita, CR=Castro Rocks, AZ=Alcatraz Island, YBI=Yerba Buena Island, NS=Newark Slough, MS=Mowry Slough, FMR=Fitzgerald Marine Reserve.

Surveys

Volunteer observers were trained to monitor harbor seals at designated sites within Point Reyes and at Point Bonita during two classroom and two field sessions in February and March 2011 (Figure 3). Many of the volunteers had been previously trained and returned to the 2011 season with several years of experience. New volunteers were required to be mentored by returning volunteers at a site before they conducted an unsupervised survey.

Figure 3. Volunteer training at Drakes Estero within Point Reyes National Seashore. NPS Photo.

Harbor seal surveys were conducted throughout the breeding (March 1st through May 31st) and molting (June 1st through July 31st) seasons once to twice per week at each Marin County location. Surveys were conducted at medium to low tides (below 3 ft) during the day. Surveys were not conducted in heavy fog because of poor visibility and they were not conducted in the rain because harbor seals haul out in lower numbers in the rain (Jemison and Pendleton 2001).

Generally, volunteers surveyed for approximately 2 hours from fixed observation points with all subsites counted approximately every 30 minutes for a total of four counts each survey. Subsites were counted and recorded separately on pre-formatted datasheets and then added for site totals every half hour. Tomales Point, Bolinas Lagoon, and Duxbury Reef often had only two counts each survey due to hiking/traveling time between subsites.

For each subsite the observer recorded the time, number of adult and immature seals, pups, dead pups, red-pelaged seals, and fresh shark-bitten seals. Red pelage is easily identified and results from the deposition of iron oxide precipitates on the hair shaft; it usually extends from the head down to the shoulder and is of interest due to its rarity outside of the San Francisco Bay Area (Allen et al. 1993). During the molting season (June-August) all animals were counted as adults or immature seals because of the difficulty in distinguishing large pups from immature seals.

On a separate data form, disturbances and potential disturbances were recorded as they occurred. Disturbances included any events that caused the seals to lift their head (head alert), flush (move towards the water), or flush into water, while potential disturbances were defined as any anthropogenic event within a defined haul-out zone that had the potential to flush seals. Observers recorded the time, source, and effect of each disturbance. The information on the effect included the reaction of the seals, the number of seals that reacted, and when and where they rehauled if they were flushed into the water. In some cases the disturbance was not directly observed, but surveyors recorded the number of animals affected with an unknown disturbance. Disturbances were recorded by fixed categories to assist with summary analyses (Table 1).

Table 1. Categories used to record disturbance sources on field datasheets.

Source	Example
Aircraft	Airplane, Helicopter, Hang glider, Ultralight
Bird	Gull, Raven, Turkey Vulture
Dog	Dog, Dog barking
Human	Clam diggers, Hiker, Horse rider, Oyster Worker, Researcher
Motor-boat	Motorboat, Jet ski
Non Motor-boat	Canoe, Kayak, Sailboat, Wind surfer
Other	Coyote, Other Pinniped, Rock Slide, etc.
Vehicle	Bus, Car, Motorcycle

On alternating weekends, regional surveys were conducted at all sites included in the regional counts (see Figure 2). Participants in the region-wide surveys included various organizations and volunteers. Regional counts could be conducted at anytime between Thursday and Monday over the selected regional survey weekends.

All count and disturbance datasheets were entered into a relational Microsoft Access database during the course of the field season. At the end of the season, the database records were error-checked against the paper datasheets for accuracy. The records were further reviewed to ensure that only accurate and complete count data were used for analysis. For example, incomplete counts or counts that may have been hampered by poor weather conditions were noted in the database as poor quality surveys and excluded from analysis.

Data Management and Analysis
Although harbor seal data were collected according to subsites at each monitoring location, subsite data are not reported or analyzed within this report. By summing the subsite counts for each survey time interval, the maximum site total was identified for each survey and used for data summaries and analyses. During the breeding months of March, April, and May, the maximum total site count for each survey included the adult/immature and pup age categories.

The maximum number of seals counted at a site over the course of the entire season is often used for comparisons between years and sites. Because there is little movement of harbor seals between sites during both the pupping and molting seasons (Lowry 2001, Nickel 2003), it was assumed that individual animals were not counted at more than one site. The maximum total count for each year within the study area was determined by taking the sum of the maximum count at each location. The maximum total count was determined separately for the breeding and molting seasons. Maximum counts at each location may have occurred on separate days (Barlow 2002). When compiling count summaries from the harbor seal data, only records noted as high quality counts were included. During the regional survey weekends, it was not uncommon for a site to be surveyed more than once. In these cases, the survey with the greater seal count was used for any regional summaries. A regional population estimate was derived from a correction factor of 1.54 calculated in central and northern California to account for seals in the water during surveys during the molt season (Harvey and Goley 2011).

The total maximum counts of breeding season adult and immature seals, pups, and molting season harbor seals were averaged separately across survey years 2000 to 2011 and compared to the 2011 data. Inclusion of all survey years in the average calculation accounts for the inherent inter-annual variability in the harbor seal population and in reproductive output. For comparisons of past regional surveys, complete data sets for the locations outside of Point Reyes are only available since 2005. Maximum counts from Bodega Marine Lab were not included in the multi-year comparisons since the site was not surveyed in recent years.

When examining disturbance events, only actual disturbances, those that elicited a head-alert or flush reaction from the seals, were used for summary analysis. Disturbance tallies were based on disturbance sources rather than the number of subsites or seals affected. Disturbance rates were calculated as the number of disturbance events that occurred during the time period from the first observation to the end of the final observation period. Because the disturbance data were not analyzed for effects on the seal count data in this report, all actual disturbance data were used for analysis regardless of the quality of the associated seal count data. Potential disturbances (events that could potentially elicit a reaction from seals) were recorded by volunteers to quantify any given type of disturbance recurring at a particular site, but this information is not analyzed in this report. These data may be used to understand potential emerging disturbance issues at each location.

The harbor seal monitoring data are dynamic and may change over time as errors are discovered and fixed, and as data analysis procedures are corrected or improved. For this reason, summary data reported here for 2000 to 2010 may differ from data summaries published in previous harbor seal reports. In particular, a thorough review and update to the disturbance data occurred since the 2007 annual harbor seal monitoring report (Truchinski et al. 2008).

Results

Overall

In 2011, 41 volunteers helped to complete 224 surveys at Marin County locations between March 1st and July 31st, with an estimated 442 hours of monitoring. Each location was surveyed between 11 and 35 times, which includes 12 regional surveys. At Marin locations, a maximum of 2,676 adults and 1,302 pups were observed during the breeding season (March-May) and 2,883 individuals were recorded during the molting season (June-July) (Table 2).

Table 2. Summary data of harbor seal colonies for the 2011 season. All reported numbers reflect the maximum number seen during a single census.

Location	Max # adults in breeding season[1]	Max # pups in breeding season	Max # seals in molting season[2]	# Surveys		Max # reds[3]	Max # shark bites[3]	Max # dead pups[3]
Bolinas Lagoon	379	192	421	Weekday:	32	12	1	1
				Weekend:	3			
Double Point	587	406	845	Weekday:	16	7	3	5
				Weekend:	12			
Drakes Estero	715	364	576	Weekday:	24	16	0	7
				Weekend:	9			
Duxbury Reef	23	4	36	Weekday:	31	0	0	0
				Weekend:	3			
Point Reyes Headlands	69	38	305	Weekday:	11	2	0	0
				Weekend:	0			
Tomales Bay	425	141	229	Weekday:	16	12	0	0
				Weekend:	10			
Tomales Point	395	145	303	Weekday:	21	2	2	3
				Weekend:	5			
Point Bonita	83	12	168	Weekday:	19	5	0	0
				Weekend:	12			
TOTAL	**2,676**	**1,302**	**2,883**		**224**	**56**	**6**	**16**

[1] Adults and immatures during the breeding season, March 1 to May 31.

[2] All age classes during the molting season, June 1 to July 31.

[3] The maximum number observed March 1 to July 31.

Adult and Pup Counts During the Breeding Season

Adults: The maximum count of adult and immature seals during the 2011 breeding season was 2,676 (Figure 4). Drakes Estero had the most adults (715), followed by Double Point (587; Table 2).

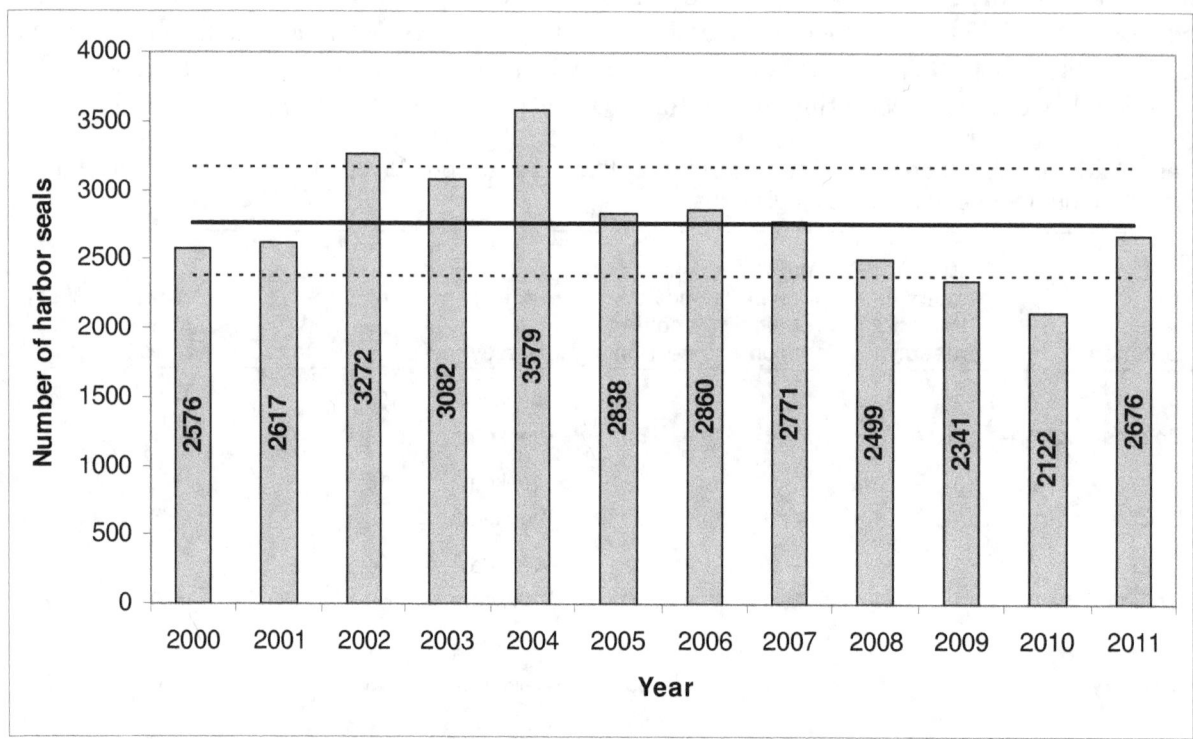

Figure 4. Maximum counts of harbor seal adults and immatures during the breeding season (March-May) for 2000-2011 at Marin County locations. The solid line on the graph represents the mean of the maximum adult counts from 2000-2011 (mean = 2,769.4) and the dashed lines represent one standard deviation from the mean (SD = 400.4).

Pups: The combined maximum pup count for all Marin County locations during the 2011 breeding season was 1,302 pups (Figure 5). This is a large increase from the 2010 season and one of the highest counts in the 12 year period of the monitoring program. Drakes Estero and Double Point accounted for 59% (770) of pups at Marin County locations, which is consistent with the proportions of pups in the past.

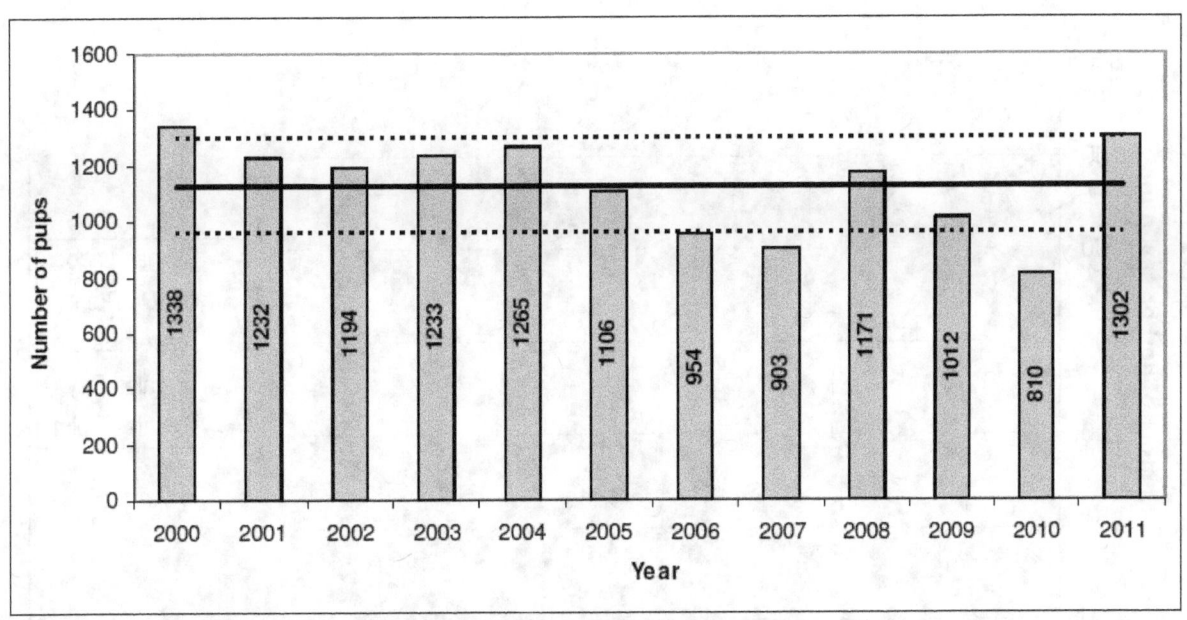

Figure 5. Maximum harbor seal pup counts for 2000-2011 at Marin County locations. The solid line on the graph represents the mean of the maximum pup counts from 2000-2011 (mean = 1,126.7), and the dashed lines represent one standard deviation from the mean (SD = 169.8).

The date of the first pup observed has been documented since 2000, and there is no apparent trend in the date or location of the first pup observed from 2000 to 2011 (Table 3). The first reported viable pup of 2011 was seen on March 16 at Drakes Estero. No other pups were seen at any other sites until over a week later at Tomales Bay on March 25.

Table 3. Date of first pup observed in the season by location, 2000-2011.

Year	Date	Location
2000	March 14	Point Reyes Headlands
2001	March 16	Tomales Bay
2002	March 3	Drakes Estero
2003	March 27	Bolinas Lagoon
2004	March 20	Double Point
2005	March 6	Drakes Estero
2006	March 9	Double Point
2007	March 2	Double Point
2008	March 16	Bolinas Lagoon
2009	March 6	Tomales Bay
2010	March 18	Tomales Bay
2011	March 16	Drakes Estero

All of the primary pupping sites of Point Reyes (Bolinas Lagoon, Double Point, Drakes Estero, Tomales Bay, and Tomales Point) increased in maximum pup numbers from 2010 to 2011 (Figure 6). Tomales Bay experienced the largest one year difference (+156%), followed by Double Point (+77%), and Drakes Estero (+63%). Point Bonita, although not a primary pupping site, should be noted as pup counts continue to steadily increase (Figure 7).

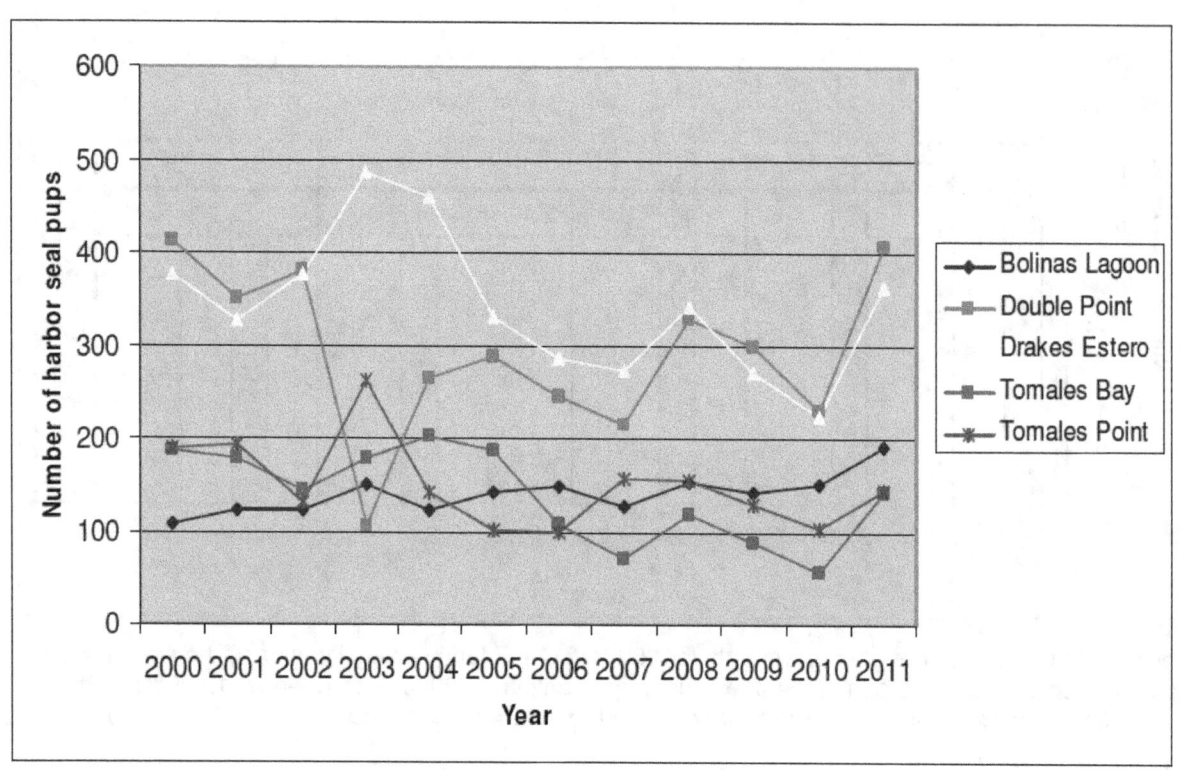

Figure 6. Maximum harbor seal pup counts at the dominant Marin County pupping locations, 2000-2011. The maximums of each site may have been observed on different days.

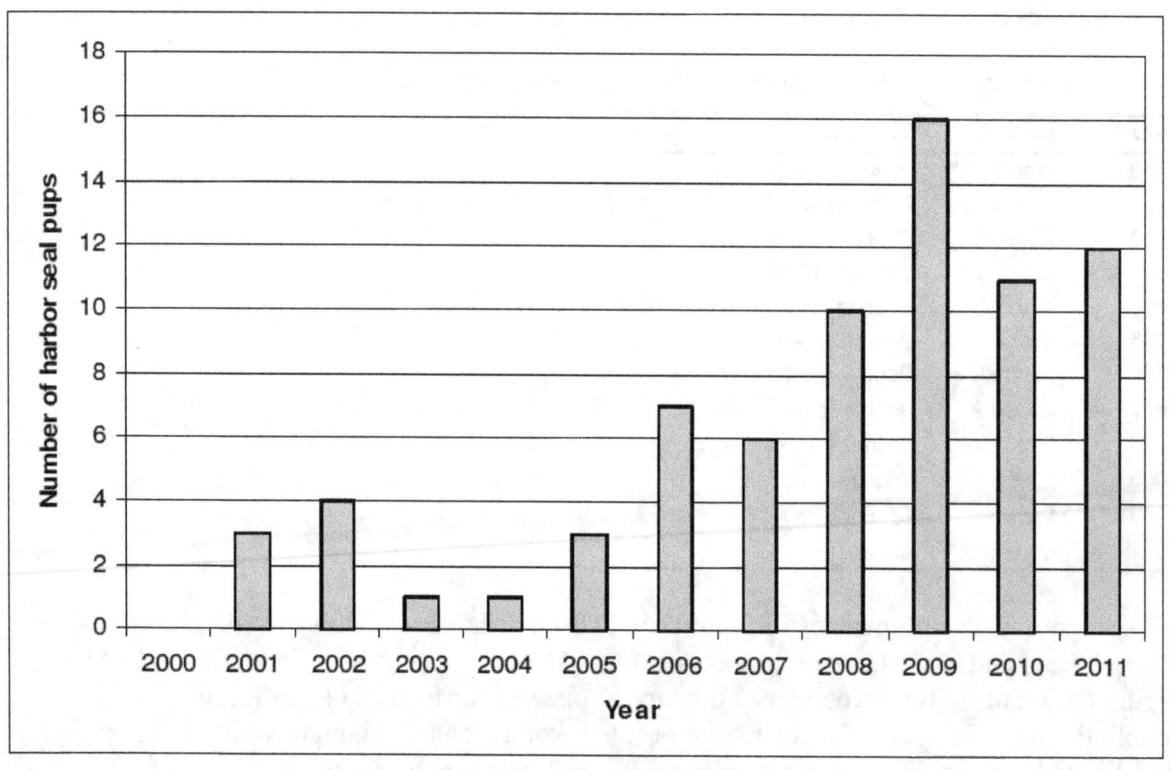

Figure 7. Maximum harbor seal pup counts at Point Bonita, 2000-2011.

Molt Counts

The maximum count of all seals during the 2011 molt season for all Marin County locations was 2,883 seals (Figure 8). Along with the 2010 season, this is the lowest recorded count in the past 12 years. Both seasons had similar maximum counts and continue the decline that has been seen in the molting season since 2005, based off a peak count in 2004. Drakes Estero and Double Point comprised 49% (1,421) of the total seals counted during the molt season (Table 2). This proportion is consistent with past years.

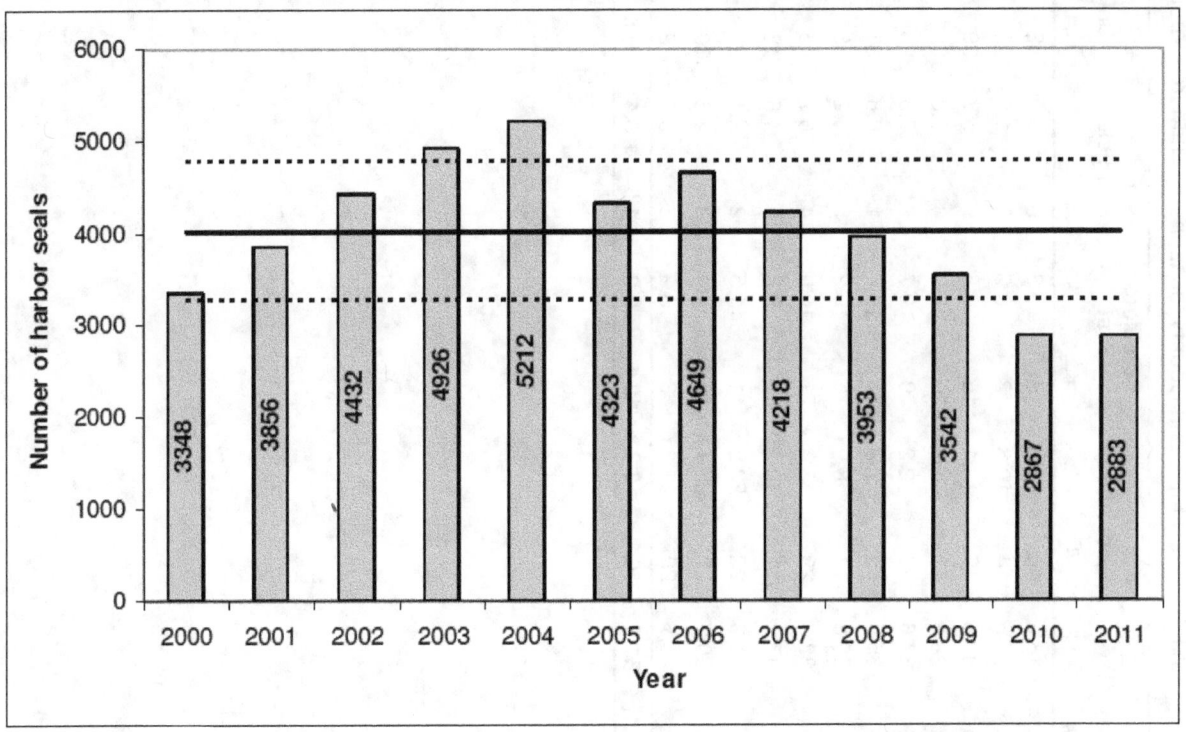

Figure 8. Maximum harbor seal counts during the molt season (June-July) for 2000-2011 at Marin County locations. The solid line on the graph represents the mean of the maximum molt counts from 2000-2011 (mean = 4,017.4) and the dashed lines represent one standard deviation from the mean (SD = 755.1).

Disturbances

At the Marin County locations in 2011, 94 disturbances were recorded that elicited a response from harbor seals (Table 4). The most common disturbance source was humans on foot (29%, Table 4). Motorboats and unknown sources were the next most common sources with 21% and 20%, respectively. These three categories are consistently the top sources of disturbances. Tomales Bay had the highest number of disturbances in 2011 with 28, followed by Drakes Estero (21). The disturbances at Tomales Bay were mostly related to passing boat traffic, whereas those at Drakes Estero were primarily caused by hikers near Limantour Beach and Drakes Beach.

13

Table 4. Identified sources of disturbances (head alert, flush, flush into water) for Marin County locations, from March through July, 2000-2011.

Year	Aircraft		Bird		Dog		Human		Motorboat		Non-Motor Boat		Vehicle		Unknown		Other		Total
	#	%	#	%	#	%	#	%	#	%	#	%	#	%	#	%	#	%	
2000	14	11.3	19	15.3	0	0.0	23	18.5	14	11.3	9	7.3	0	0.0	43	34.7	2	1.6	124
2001	4	3.1	9	6.9	1	0.8	45	34.6	14	10.8	12	9.2	2	1.5	28	21.5	15	11.5	130
2002	9	5.7	11	7.0	0	0.0	48	30.6	19	12.1	15	9.6	9	5.7	39	24.8	7	4.5	157
2003	10	7.5	10	7.5	0	0.0	38	28.6	13	9.8	20	15.0	3	2.3	32	24.1	7	5.3	133
2004	2	2.2	7	7.5	1	1.1	35	37.6	2	2.2	9	9.7	7	7.5	23	24.7	7	7.5	93
2005	10	8.1	10	8.1	2	1.6	43	35.0	9	7.3	14	11.4	1	0.8	31	25.2	3	2.4	123
2006	8	5.1	13	8.3	1	0.6	57	36.3	14	8.9	16	10.2	5	3.2	35	22.3	8	5.1	157
2007	14	6.7	13	6.2	2	1.0	70	33.3	29	13.8	21	10.0	14	6.7	45	21.4	2	1.0	210
2008	4	3.7	5	4.6	0	0.0	51	47.2	11	10.2	10	9.3	5	4.6	18	16.7	4	3.7	108
2009	3	3.1	6	6.3	0	0.0	21	21.9	22	22.9	11	11.5	2	2.1	27	28.1	4	4.2	96
2010	5	4.4	5	4.4	6	1.8	35	30.7	27	23.7	5	4.4	3	2.6	30	26.3	2	1.8	114
2011	5	5.3	11	11.7	0	0.0	27	28.7	20	21.3	3	3.2	3	3.2	19	20.2	6	6.4	94
Mean	7.3	5.5	9.9	7.8	0.6	0.6	41.1	31.9	16.2	12.8	12.1	9.2	4.5	3.4	30.8	24.2	5.6	4.6	128

The rate of disturbances per hour in 2011 was highest for Tomales Bay (0.59 disturbances/hr), followed by Bolinas Lagoon (0.32 disturbances/hr) and Drakes Estero (0.27 disturbances/hr; Figure 9). Of the sites that regularly have more than five disturbances per season, Drakes Estero experienced the greatest change compared with 2010 with a 28% decrease in the disturbance rate (Figure 10). Decreases in disturbance rates were also seen at Tomales Bay (-20%), Bolinas Lagoon (-18%), and Double Point (-17%). The rates of disturbances vary from year to year depending on activities at each location, but trends have not been analyzed.

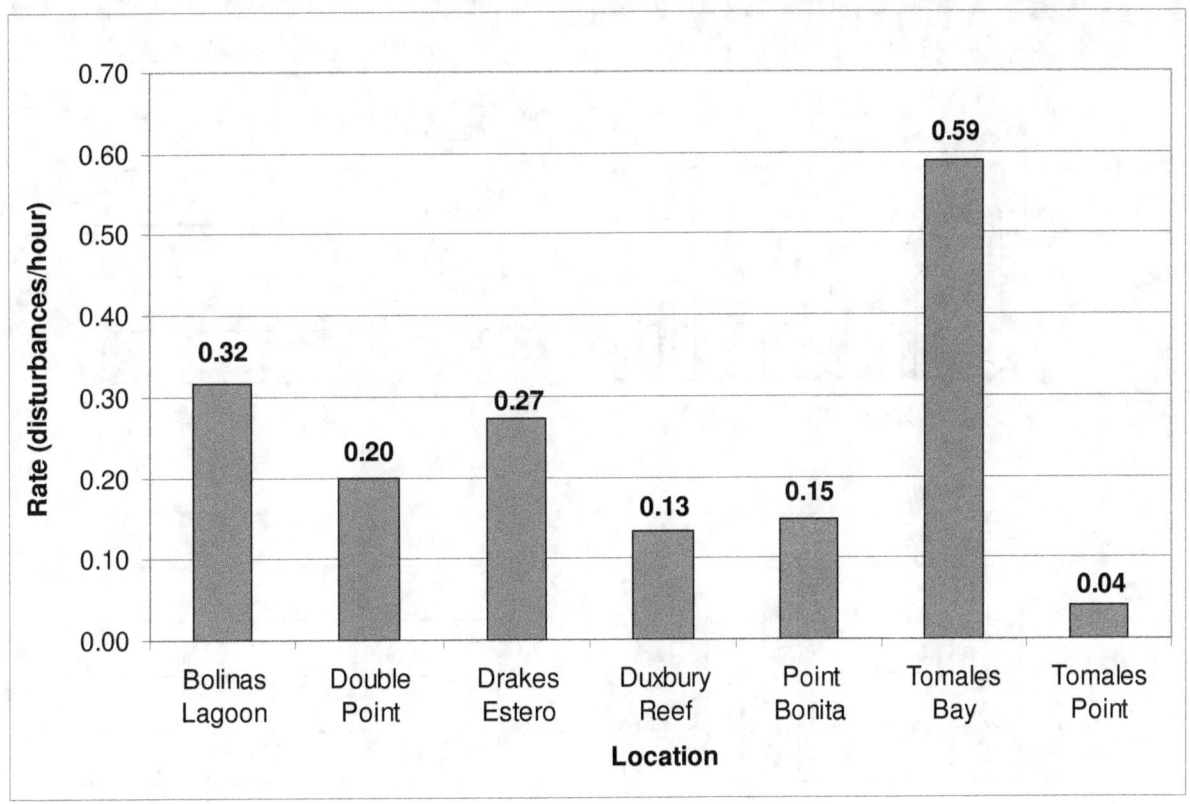

Figure 9. Rates of disturbances per hour at Marin County locations from March 1st through July 31st, 2011. Only actual disturbances (head alert, flush, flush water) were used and survey time was based on observation time for all complete surveys (with or without disturbances).

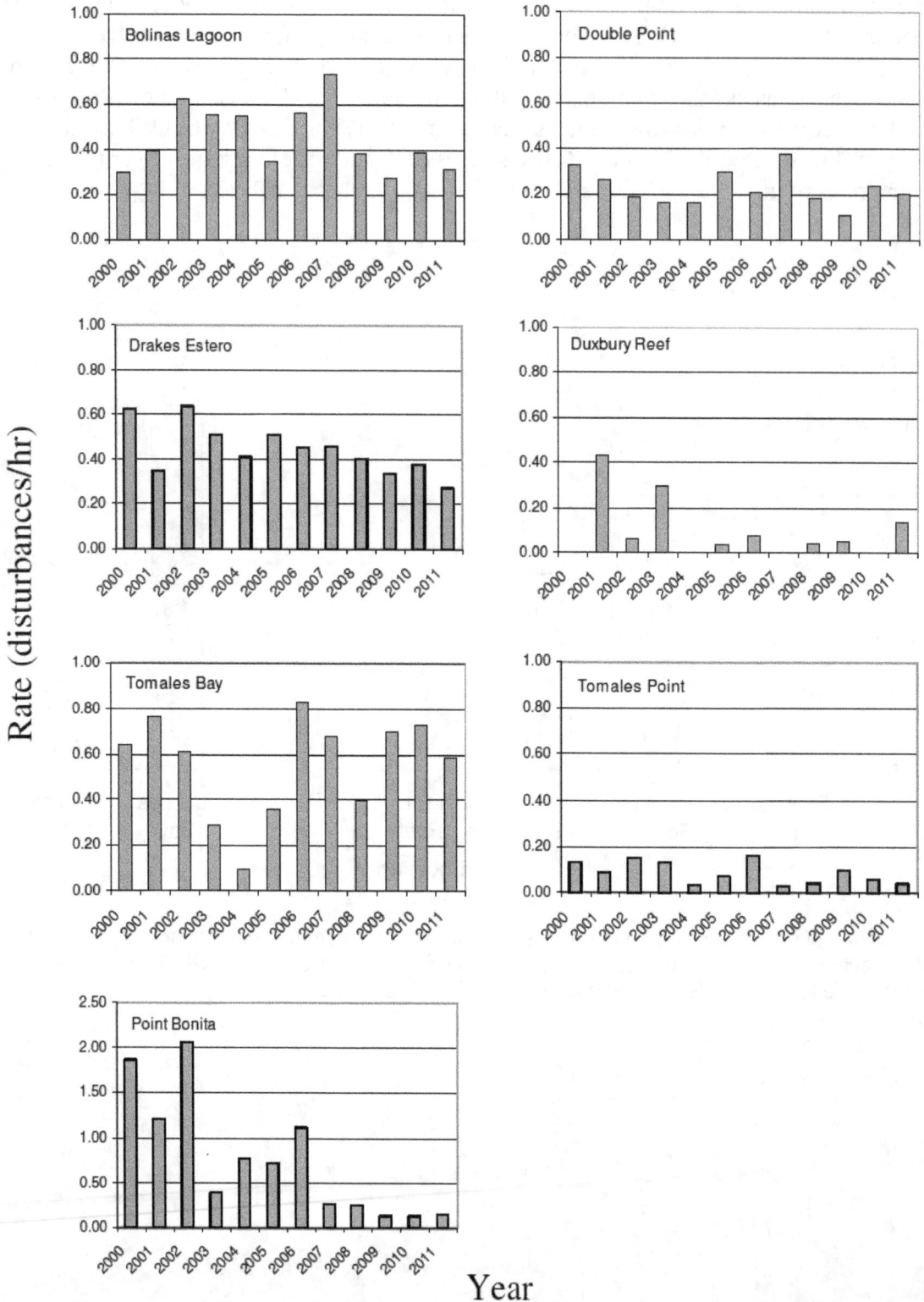

Figure 10. Rates of disturbances per hour at Marin County locations from March through July of 2000-2011. Only actual disturbances (head alert, flush, flush water) were used, and survey time was based on observation time for all complete surveys (with or without disturbances). Note change in rate scale for Point Bonita.

Summary by Site

Bolinas Lagoon

Bolinas Lagoon had 35 complete surveys between March 1st and July 31st, 2011. Of those, surveys, 32 were on weekdays and 3 were on weekends. The maximum count during the breeding season had 379 adults and 192 pups. The first viable pup was recorded on March 28th. During the molting season, the maximum count was 421 seals (Table 2). Bolinas had a similar number of disturbances recorded as in 2010. The primary cause of disturbances was humans on foot, which included visitors and fishermen. This site is along scenic Highway 1 and many people stop to visit the area. The 2011 disturbance rate for Bolinas Lagoon slightly decreased from 2010 (0.39 to 0.32 disturbances/hr; Figure 10).

Double Point

Double Point had 28 complete surveys between March 1st and July 31st, 2011. Of those, 16 were on weekdays and 12 were on weekends. The maximum count during the breeding season was 587 adults and 406 pups. The first pups were recorded on March 31st, when 13 were seen. The molting season yielded a maximum count of 845 seals (Table 2). Double Point experienced disturbances which were primarily caused by unknown sources, but some were also caused by rock slides. Unknown disturbances may have been caused by small rockslides from the eroding cliffs above the beaches that observers could not see or hear. The disturbance rate in 2011 had a small decrease from 2010 (0.24 to 0.20 disturbances/hr; Figure 10).

Drakes Estero

The Drakes Estero complex which includes the Limantour Spit had 33 complete surveys between March 1st and July 31st, 2011. Of those, 24 were on weekdays and 9 were on weekends. The maximum count during the breeding season was 715 adults and 364 pups and the maximum molt count was 576 (Table 2). The first viable pup of the season out of all the Marin County locations was recorded here on March 16th. This year had the lowest number of disturbances recorded at this site during the 12 year period and the disturbance rate was lower than 2010 (0.38 to 0.27 disturbances/hr; Figure 10). The majority of disturbances were caused by hikers on Limantour and Drakes Beaches due to easy accessibility. In past years, seals hauled out at the mouth of Drakes Estero on isolated sandbars were rarely disturbed by hikers on Drakes Beach. However, this year during low tides, the beach was connected to the isolated sandbars in the mouth of the estero, which allowed hikers to approach the seals. On one occasion, a bald eagle (*Haliaeetus leucocephalus*) was seen on a haul-out site which caused other birds to react and, as a result, the seals flushed. The estero is seasonally closed to kayaking from March to June during the critical pupping period and no kayaks were reported during this time.

Duxbury Reef

Duxbury Reef had 34 complete surveys between March 1st and July 31st, 2011. Of those, 31 were on weekdays and 3 were on weekends. During the breeding season, the maximum adult count was 23 and the maximum pup count was 4, while during the molting season the maximum seal count was 36 (Table 2). The first day a pup was recorded at this site was on April 26th. This is not a regular pupping site and pups seen here might have come from other locations such as Bolinas Lagoon. Duxbury had the lowest number of seals and only three disturbances were recorded there. Two were caused by tidepoolers and one was an unknown source. Disturbances are rarely recorded at Duxbury Reef, possibly due to the poor accessibility of the location.

17

Point Bonita

Point Bonita had 31 complete surveys between March 1st and July 31st, 2011. Of those, 19 were on weekdays and 12 were on weekends. During the breeding season, the maximum count was 83 adults and 12 pups and the maximum molt count was 168 (Table 2). The first pups were seen on April 18th. The maximum pup count has been increasing over the past few years. The disturbances at Point Bonita were primarily caused by motorboats, which included fishing and sightseeing boats. There has been a decrease in disturbances caused by humans since the area below the paved walkway was closed to visitors in mid-June 2007. During 2011, there was only one reported case of people in the closed area. It is unknown if there was a disturbance because they were already there when the observer arrived and no seals were present. Point Bonita disturbance rate was similar to last year (0.14 and 0.15 disturbances/hr, respectively; Figure 10).

Point Reyes Headlands

Point Reyes Headlands had 11 complete surveys between March 1st and July 31st, 2011. All of the surveys were completed during weekdays. During the breeding season, the maximum adult count was 69 and the maximum pup count was 38, while during the molting season the maximum seal count was 305 (Table 2). The estimated date of the first viable pups is not reliable because of the low amount of surveys completed at this site. There was one recorded disturbance at the Point Reyes Headlands which was caused by an unknown source. This site rarely has disturbances because of its remoteness and inaccessibility. Most of the harbor seals were seen at a large northern elephant seal (*Mirounga angustirostris*) colony pocket beach.

Tomales Bay

Tomales Bay had 26 complete surveys between March 1st and July 31st, 2011. Of those, 16 were weekday and 10 were weekend surveys. During the breeding season, the maximum adult count was 425 and the maximum pup count was 141, while during the molting season the maximum seal count was 229 (Table 2). The first viable pup at this site was recorded on March 25th. The majority of the disturbances were caused by motorboats traveling around the sandbars, as well as a few incidences where boats landed at the haul-out site and caused seals to flush. There were also many disturbances caused by people clamming near the seals, as the sandbars in Tomales Bay are a very popular spot for recreational clamming. During many of the weekend surveys, when clammers are out in higher numbers, there were multiple disturbances during a single survey. Tomales Bay had the highest number of disturbances and the highest disturbance rate of all locations in 2011 (0.59; Figure 9). However, there was a decrease in the disturbance rate from 2010 (0.73 to 0.59; Figure 10).

Tomales Point

Tomales Point had 26 complete surveys between March 1st and July 31st, 2011. Of those, 21 were on weekdays and 5 were on weekends. During the breeding season, the maximum adult count was 395 and the maximum pup count was 145, while during the molting season the maximum seal count was 303 (Table 2). The first pups were recorded at this site on April 11th, when 6 pups were seen. Tomales Point experienced a small number of disturbances, primarily caused by abalone divers and a harbor seal researcher walking along the bluff during a survey. Due to its remoteness, however, the Tomales Point location is generally not frequented by visitors. Abalone divers are generally the only people seen near the seal haul-out sites. However, due to the distance between Tomales Point subsites, observers cannot stay in one location long enough to see if the divers cause any disturbances. On two occasions, people were seen near a seal haul-out site, but no seals were present at the time.

Regional Sites

Twelve regional surveys occurred between March 10th and August 1st, 2011 at 22 different locations. Not all sites were surveyed on all scheduled days due to weather conditions or scheduling conflicts. During the breeding season, a maximum of 3,858 adults and 1,532 pups were observed, although the maximum counts may have occurred on different days for each location (Table 5). During the molting season, the combined maximum count of all seals from each site was 4,226. Marin County locations accounted for 69% of the maximum adult and immature seal breeding count, 84% of the maximum pup count, and 65% of the maximum molt count. A population estimate for the regional population of harbor seals for the molt season was 6,508 based on a correction factor of 1.54 (1.54*4,226) (Harvey and Goley 2011). All counties experienced an increase in numbers from 2010 to 2011 for both the breeding and molting seasons, except San Mateo and Marin Counties during the molting season, which had numbers similar to last year (Figures 11 and 12).

In Sonoma County during the breeding season, the Sonoma Coast had the high counts of adult and immature seals and pups, followed by Jenner. In the molting season, Jenner had the high count of seals. Within the San Francisco Bay, high counts for seals occurred at Castro Rocks in both seasons. In past years, Yerba Buena Island and Mowry Slough had high counts as well, however, this year both sites reported lower numbers. In San Mateo County, the highest concentration of seals was at Fitzgerald Marine Reserve during both seasons. This season there were multiple locations that had maximum counts in early March: Sonoma Coast, Jenner, Castro Rocks, and Fitzgerald Marine Reserve. These counts were not included since they did not fall within the expected range of the peak breeding season. These early peaks most likely included seals that were still moving in and out of areas.

The majority of the disturbances in Sonoma County this year were recorded at Bodega Marine Reserve, with the source being people in the area. In San Francisco Bay, the majority of disturbances were reported at Alcatraz, with sources of aircraft and motorboats. In San Mateo County, only Fitzgerald Marine Reserve experienced a disturbance, which was caused by fishermen.

Table 5. Regional surveys of harbor seal numbers in central California, March 10th through August 1st, 2011. Twelve surveys were scheduled on alternating weekends, seven during the breeding season and five during the molt. Values reported as mean, standard error (SE), and maximum (Max).

Location	N	Breeding Season Adult mean	SE	Adult max[1]	Pup max[2]	N	Molting Season Mean	SE	Max
Sonoma County									
Sonoma Coast[3]	7	137.2	22.9	211	54	5	158.6	20.8	224
Jenner	7	118.0	22.6	185	13	5	230.4	36.5	345
Bodega Marine Reserve	7	25.4	4.5	43	11	3	51.7	3.7	59
Marin County									
Tomales Bay	7	318.6	26.9	425	131	5	111.8	41.3	229
Tomales Point[3]	7	230.3	41.2	395	145	5	219.4	21.0	275
Point Reyes Headland[3]	6	51.2	6.6	69	38	5	126.4	46.2	305
Drakes Estero	7	440.4	73.7	715	364	4	519.8	27.0	576
Double Point	7	311.4	72.2	587	409	5	507.2	99.9	845
Duxbury Reef	7	14.4	3.4	23	2	5	6.6	4.0	21
Bolinas Lagoon	7	228.6	28.0	379	192	5	266.8	39.5	379
Point Bonita	7	42.7	9.8	74	12	5	92.8	4.0	107
San Francisco Bay									
Alcatraz	7	2.9	1.1	7	0	5	7.8	2.1	12
Castro Rocks	7	126.8	2.5	137	37	5	129.4	5.3	139
Yerba Buena Island	7	41.9	7.7	61	8	5	60.8	7.6	84
Newark Slough	2	45.5	5.5	51	11	3	13.0	8.1	28
Mowry Slough	2	79.0	2.0	81	12	3	59.7	14.0	87
San Mateo County									
Point San Pedro	6	8.3	3.7	23	0	3	17.3	2.7	20
Cowell Ranch	6	58.7	12.1	106	18	5	78.4	22.8	130
Pescadero	7	26.9	3.0	35	10	5	30.6	2.6	37
Pebble Beach	7	38.4	4.8	58	10	5	76.0	8.5	104
Bean Hollow	7	2.3	1.8	13	0	5	0.0	0.0	0
Fitzgerald Marine Reserve	7	143.2	8.3	180	55	5	173.0	17.0	220
ALL SITES				**3,858**	**1,532**				**4,226**

[1]Based on the total for a single day.

[2]Based on the total for the same single day as above

[3]Includes surveys that occurred outside of regional weekend period

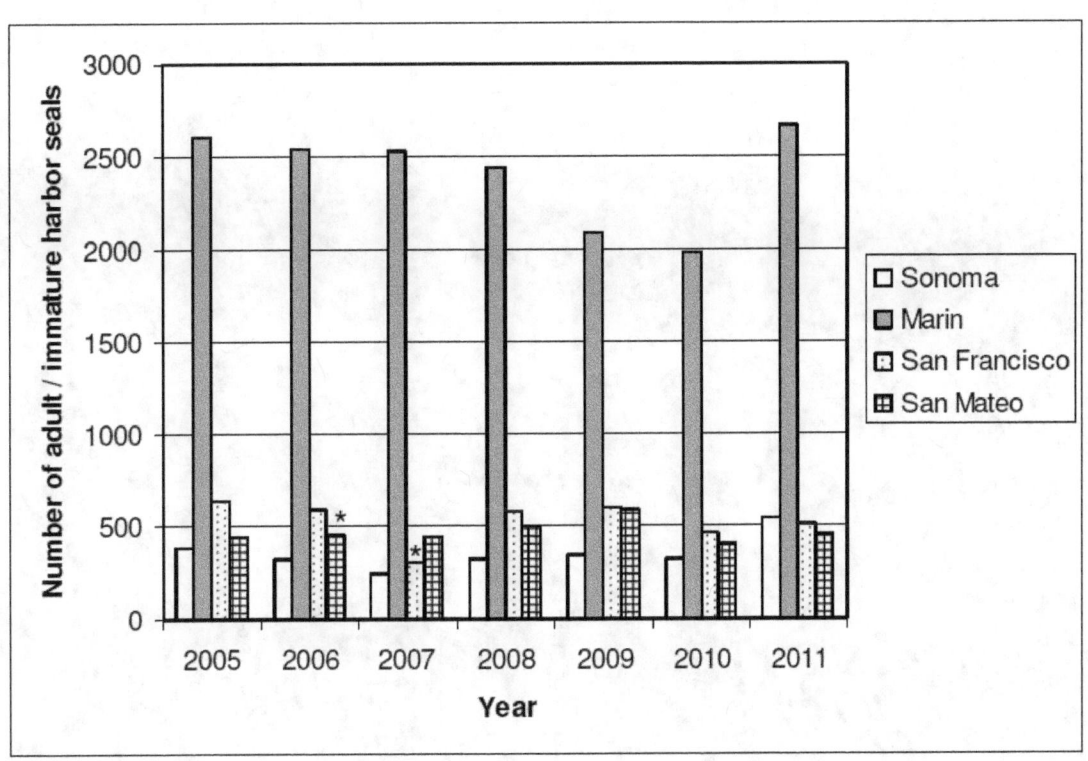

Figure 11. Maximum counts of harbor seal adults and immatures during the breeding season for the 2005-2011 regional surveys in central California. * Incomplete surveys conducted for San Mateo County in 2006 and San Francisco County in 2007.

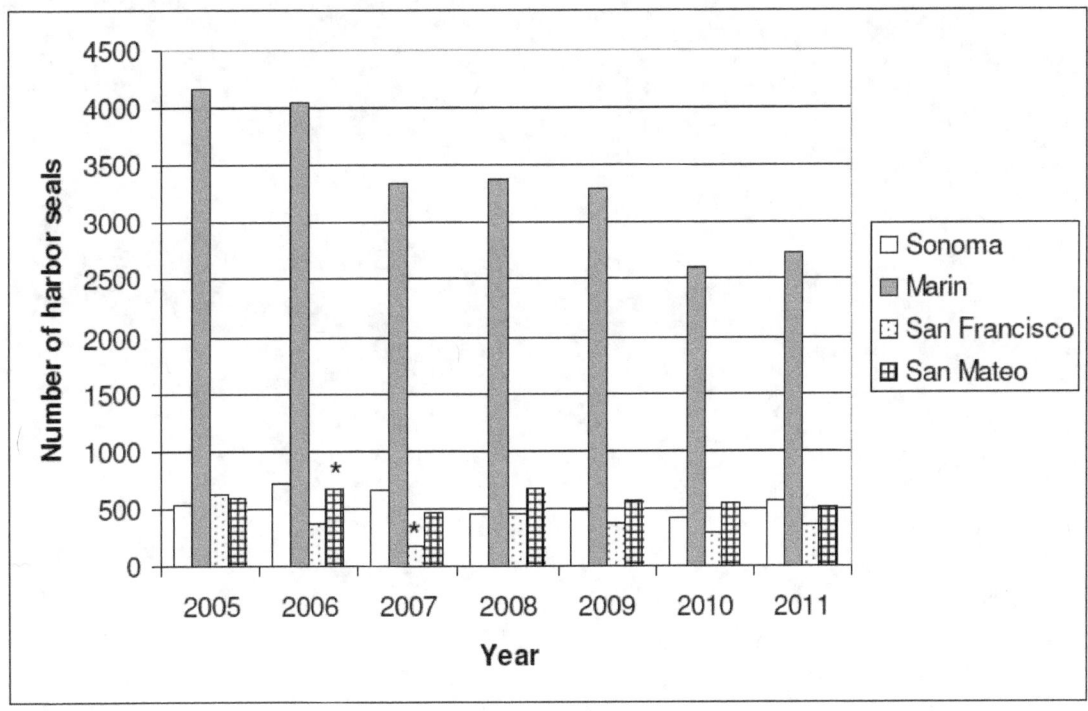

Figure 12. Maximum counts of all age classes of harbor seals during the molting season for the 2005-2011 regional surveys in central California. * Incomplete surveys conducted for San Mateo County in 2006 and San Francisco County in 2007.

Discussion

Harbor seals are apex predators of the marine ecosystem and numerous, interacting, dynamic processes have the potential to affect their abundance and distribution. Harbor seals are sensitive to changes in the marine ecosystem and respond quickly to changes in prey abundance and distribution, and to human disturbance (Allen et al. 1985; Thompson and Miller 1990; Trillmich and Ono 1991; Thompson et al. 1998; Sydeman and Allen 1999). Information gained at Point Reyes National Seashore and Golden Gate National Recreation Area contributes to predicting how recovered populations will influence the ecosystem structure and productivity of this region. Studying trends and alterations in habitat also may provide insights into the potential or real effects of climate change on harbor seal distribution and abundance.

In 2010, the maximum counts of adult and immature seals and pups in the breeding season were the lowest numbers recorded between 2000 and 2010. In 2011, both counts increased. The 2011 adult and immature seal count is similar to the mean of the 12 year period, while the pup count of 2011 is one of the highest counts recorded since 2000. The maximum count during the molting season of 2010 was also the lowest recorded in the study period and the count from 2011 has remained as low. The molting season numbers appear to have declined since 2005; however, more intense analysis is required to determine if this decrease is biologically or statistically significant.

From 2000 to 2011, Drakes Estero and Double Point annually produced the highest numbers of harbor seal pups. In 2011, these two sites combined produced 59% of the pups observed at Marin County sites. A similar pattern is seen during the molting season, with these two sites comprising 49% of the seals recorded in 2011. These two sites remain important breeding and molting sites for the seals. Tomales Bay, which has seen low pup numbers in recent years, had a substantial increase in the number of pups recorded. This site had many disturbances reported; however, the majority of disturbances took place during the molting season and would not have disrupted the critical female and pup bonding and nursing period.

Among Marin County locations, the time period during the breeding season when the maximum amount of adult and immature seals and pups was seen at each site was clustered around 3 weeks during the end of April and beginning of May; except for three non-primary breeding sites (Duxbury Reef, Point Bonita, and Point Reyes Headlands) which had early maximum counts at the beginning of March. We did not include these counts since they likely represent seals that are still moving to breeding areas. During the molting season, the peak at each site was more spread out and occurred at various times between the beginning of June and middle of July. It is possible that this might have resulted in individual seals being counted more than once at different sites during the molting season. However, this would not change the overall result of this year having one of the lowest molt counts in the past 12 years. The low count may be explained, in part, by seals either spending more time foraging after the energetically intensive breeding season or by their departure from the area. An intensive analysis, though, would be required to determine the cause for this decline.

Oceanographic conditions in the summer of 2010 through the winter of 2011 were some of the coldest ocean waters seen in recent years, following the 2009-2010 El Niño event, which receded in April of 2010. Additionally, the winter ichthyoplankton biomass was higher in 2010 and in stark contrast to 2009 and 1998, both El Niño years (Figure 13). Such conditions possibly were favorable for higher than average pupping rates in 2011.

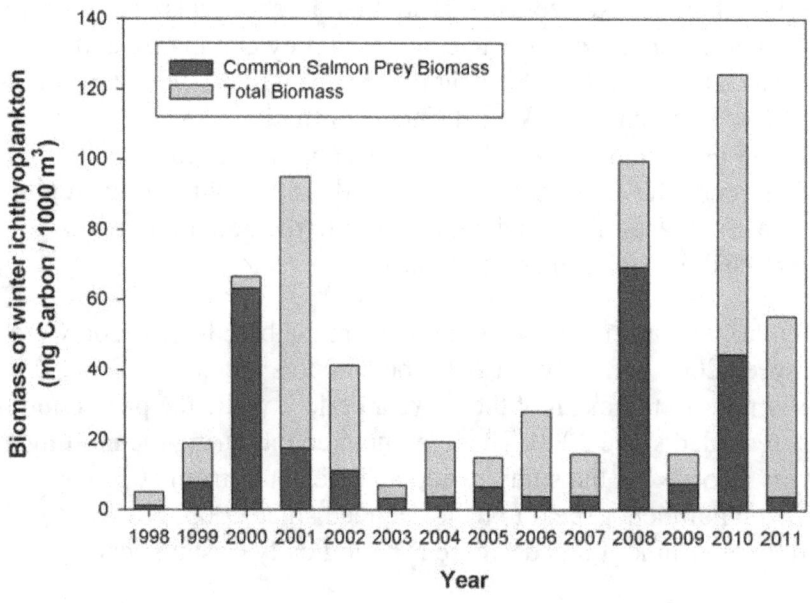

Figure 13. Ichthyoplankton winter biomass per year (NOAA 2011). Note higher than average biomass in 2010 compared to 2009.

The 2011 season had one of the lowest counts of disturbances in the 12 year period for which data were collected consistently. However, the low number of weekend surveys at half of the sites might have biased this number as more human activity is expected on weekends. Throughout the study area from 2000-2011, the primary sites that experienced disturbances were Bolinas Lagoon, Double Point, Drakes Estero, Point Bonita, and Tomales Bay. Disturbances at Point Bonita have decreased since the area was closed to visitors in mid-June 2007. In 2011, Tomales Bay had the highest number of disturbances recorded for the year, with the majority being caused by motorboats. Motorboats tend to disturb seals when they are too close in distance to the seals or when the boats are louder than normal background noise (Codde, pers. obs.). This year there were more direct disturbances caused by motorboats as a few landed at haul-out sites and stayed there for extended amounts of time preventing seals from re-hauling onshore. The most common source category of disturbance for all Marin County locations combined in 2011 was human on foot, particularly hikers and clammers. This is consistent with previous years. The next most common disturbance categories were motorboats and unknown. The unknown source category is used when the surveyor observes seals displaying a disturbance response, such as head alert, flush towards water, or flush into water, but the source cannot be identified.

One note of interest this year was a tsunami that occurred along the Pacific Coast on March 11, 2011 as a result of an earthquake in Japan. The tsunami height was predicted to be about 1.35 m in Point Reyes (NGDC/WDC 2011). Bolinas Lagoon, Duxbury Reef, Point Bonita, and Tomales Bay were surveyed during the day of the event. At Bolinas Lagoon, the only change obvious to the observer was that the tide seemed higher than expected. The survey at Duxbury reported only one seal hauled out on the reef. The observer at Point Bonita reported large waves and many seals in the water, with few hauled out. The most obvious effects of the tsunami were seen in Tomales Bay where the alternating rising and falling of the water in the bay continued throughout the entire survey; however, the seals that were hauled out did not appear disrupted by this wave action and counts stayed fairly constant during the survey.

Collaborations

NPS staff assisted graduate students of Moss Landing Marine Laboratories under the guidance of Dr. James Harvey on multiple health and movement studies of harbor seals along the central California coast. One study investigated if harbor seals were suffering from chronic selenium toxicity. A second study identified species and strains of potentially pathogenic bacteria, *Vibrio* spp., isolated from harbor seals. The third study was looking at movement and survival of post-partum harbor seals.

NPS staff and volunteers collaborated with The Marine Mammal Center on a neonatal harbor seal mortality study at Drakes Estero. NPS staff also assisted with training of volunteers monitoring harbor seals for the Stewards of the Coast and Redwoods Seal Watch program. Lastly, the central California coast regional surveys are collaborations with multiple government agencies, universities, and non-profit groups including the US Fish and Wildlife Service, Moss Landing Marine Laboratories, University of California at Davis, Farallones National Marine Sanctuary Association, The Marine Mammal Center, and Stewards of the Coast and Redwoods Seal Watch program.

Season Highlights
- A maximum of 2,676 adult and immature seals were counted onshore during the breeding season.
  - The greatest number of adults hauled out at Drakes Estero (715), followed by Double Point (587).

- A maximum of 1,302 pups were observed at Marin colonies.
  - This count is one of the highest pup counts between 2000 and 2011.
  - Drakes Estero and Double Point accounted for 59% (770) of pups at Marin colonies.

- A maximum of 2,883 animals were counted during the molting season at Marin County haul-out sites.
  - Along with the 2010 season, this is the lowest count recorded between 2000 and 2011.
  - Drakes Estero and Double Point accounted for 49% (1,421) of the total seals counted during the molt season.

- 94 disturbances were recorded during surveys.
  - The most frequent disturbance categories were humans on foot (29%), motorboat (21%), and unknown (20%).
  - Most disturbances (28) and the highest rate of disturbance (0.59 disturbances/hour) occurred at Tomales Bay.

- A small tsunami occurred on the Pacific coast and was witnessed at several Marin County seal haul-out sites.

- Regional surveys occurred 12 times throughout the breeding and molt seasons, which include Sonoma, Marin, San Francisco, and San Mateo counties. Nineteen volunteers participated in these surveys.
    - Marin County locations accounted for 69% of breeding season adult and immature seals, 84% of pups, and 65% of seals during the molting season.

- 41 volunteers completed 224 surveys at Marin County locations between March 1st and July 31st 2011, contributing approximately 442 survey hours.

Literature Cited

Adams, D., S. Allen, J. Bjork, M. Cooprider, A. Fesnock, M. Koenen, T. Leatherman, S. O'Neil, D. Press, D. Schirokauer, B. Welch, and B. Witcher. 2006. San Francisco Bay Area Network vital signs monitoring plan. NPS/SFAN/NRR 2006/017. National Park Service, Fort Collins, Colorado.

Adams, D., D. Press, M. Hester, H. Nevins, D. Roberts, B. Becker, H. Jensen, E. Flynn, M. Koenen, and S. Allen. 2009. San Francisco Bay Area Network pinniped monitoring protocol. Natural Resource Report NPS/SFAN/NRR—2009/170. National Park Service, Fort Collins, Colorado.

Allen, S. G. 1988. The movement and activity patterns of harbor seals in Drakes Estero, California. M.S. thesis, University of California, Berkeley, California. 69 pp.

Allen, S. G. and H. R. Huber. 1984. Human/pinniped interactions in the Point Reyes/Farallon Islands National Marine Sanctuary. Final Report to U. S. Dept. of Commerce, Sanctuary Programs Office. 27 pp.

Allen, S. G., D. G. Ainley, G. W. Page, and C. A. Ribic. 1985. The effect of disturbance on harbor seal haul out patterns at Bolinas Lagoon, California, 1978-1979. U.S. Fishery Bulletin 82:493-500.

Allen, S. G., H. R. Huber, C. A. Ribic, and D. G. Ainley. 1989. Population dynamics of harbor seals in the Gulf of the Farallones, California. California Fish & Game 75:224–232.

Allen, S. G., M. Stephenson, R. W. Risebrough, L. Fancher, A. Shiller, and D. Smith. 1993. Red-pelaged harbor seals of the San Francisco Bay Region. Journal of Mammology 74(3):588–593.

Allen, S., S. Waber, W. Holter, and D. Press. 2004. Long-term monitoring of harbor seals at Point Reyes, five year annual report, 1997–2001. National Park Service, Point Reyes National Seashore, Point Reyes Station, California.

Barlow, J. 2002. Report of the California harbor seal workshop, March 28–29, 2002, Southwest Fisheries Science Center. National Marine Fisheries Service, Southwest Fisheries Science Center, La Jolla, California.

Becker, B.H., D.T. Press, and S.G. Allen. 2011. Evidence for long-term spatial displacement of breeding and pupping harbor seals by shellfish aquaculture over three decades. Aquatic Conserv: Mar. Freshw. Ecosystems 21:247-260.

California Department of Fish and Game. 2009. Master Plan for the north Central Coast MPA. Appendix G. http://www.dfg.ca.gov/mlpa/draftdocuments.asp

Chan, G. L. 1979. California marine waters: Areas of Special Biological Significance, Reconnaissance Survey Report. Double Point. California State Water Resources Control Board. Division of Planning and Research. Water Quality Monitoring Report No. 79-15.

Harvey, J. T. 1987. Population dynamics, annual food consumption, movements, and dive behaviors of harbor seals, *Phoca vitulina richardsi*, in Oregon. Ph.D. Dissertation. Oregon State University, Corvallis, Oregon. 177 pp.

Harvey, J. T. and D. Goley. 2011. Determining a correction factor for aerial surveys of harbor seals in California. Marine Mammal Science 27(4):719-735.

Jemison, L. A. and G. W. Pendleton. 2001. Harbor seal population trends and factors influencing counts on Tugidak Island, Alaska. Pages 31–52 in Harbor Seal Investigations in Alaska. Annual Report for NOAA Award NA87FX0300. Alaska Department of Fish and Game. Division of Wildlife Conservation, Anchorage, Alaska. 356 pp.

Lowry, L. F., K. J. Frost, J. M. Ver Hoef and R. A. DeLong. 2001. Movements of satellite tagged subadult and adult harbor seals in Prince William Sound, Alaska. Marine Mammal Science 17:835-861.

Lowry, M. S., J. V. Carretta, and K. A. Forney. 2005. Pacific harbor seal, *Phoca vitulina richardsi*, census in California during May–July 2004. Administrative Report LJ-05-06, available from Southwest Fisheries Science Center, 8604 La Jolla Shores Drive, La Jolla, CA 92037. 38 pp.

NOAA Northwest Fisheries Science Center. Available at http://www.nwfsc.noaa.gov/research/divisions/fed/oeip/db-coastal-upwelling-index.cfm (accessed 6 October 2011).

National Geophysical Data Center / World Data Center (NGDC/WDC) Historical Tsunami Database, Boulder, CO, USA. 2011. Available at http://www.ngdc.noaa.gov/hazard/tsu_db.shtml (accessed 16 September 2011).

National Park Service Organic Act, 16 U.S.C. 1 et seq. (1988), Aug. 25, 1916, Ch. 408, 39 Stat. 535. Washington D.C.

National Park Service Omnibus Management Act, Pub. L. No. 105-391, Nov. 13, 1998, 112 Stat. 3498. National Park Service Management Policies. 2001. U.S. Department of Interior, National Park Service. Washington D.C.

National Park Service. 2010. Annual Park Visitation Report. Available at www.nature.nps.gov/stats/ (accessed 8 September 2011).

Nickle, B. A. 2003. Movement and Habitat Use Patterns of Harbor seals in the San Francisco Estuary, California. MS Thesis, San Francisco State University, San Francisco, California. 121 pp.

Sydeman, W. J. and S. G. Allen. 1999. Pinniped population dynamics in central California: Correlations with sea surface temperature and upwelling indices. Marine Mammal Science 15(2):446–461.

Thompson, P. M. 1987. The effect of seasonal changes in behavior on the distribution and abundance of common seals, *Phoca vitulina*, in Orkney. Ph.D. Dissertation. University of Aberdeen, England. 167 pp.

Thompson P. M., A. Mackay, D. J. Tollit, S. Enderby, and P. S. Hammond. 1998. The influence of body size and sex on the characteristics of harbour seal foraging trips. Candadian Journal of Zoology 76:1044-1053.

Thompson P. M. and D. Miller. 1990. Summer foraging activity and movements of radio-tagged seals (*Phoca vitulina*) in the Moray Firth, Scotland. Journal of Applied Ecology 27:492-501.

Trillmich, F. and C. Ono (eds). 1991. Pinnipeds and El Niño. Springer-Verlag, Berlin.

Truchinski K., E. Flynn, D. Press, D. Roberts, and S. Allen. 2008. Pacific harbor seal (*Phoca vitulina richardii)* monitoring at Point Reyes National Seashore and Golden Gate National Recreation Area: 2007 annual report. Natural Resource Technical Report NPS/SFAN/NRTR—2008/118. National Park Service, Fort Collins, Colorado.

The Department of the Interior protects and manages the nation's natural resources and cultural heritage; provides scientific and other information about those resources; and honors its special responsibilities to American Indians, Alaska Natives, and affiliated Island Communities.

NPS 641/116303, 612/116303, August 2012